Please read

'Tabula Rasa' in mind ...

However, Christopher, you were correct when you said, "Man-made religion poisons everything."

This book is for the millions of people who bought or listened online to Christopher Hitchens' book, "*god Is Not Great: How Religion Poisons Everything*" and the millions of people worldwide who watched the debates on the BBC broadcasts and YouTube videos.

# *Acknowledgements*

This book would not be available to you without the help from the following people. To them I offer my most sincere appreciation.

- Lisa Gobel
- Linda Cashdan wordpro.com
- John Piper
- Jim Helling
- Cynthia Graff
- A. A. Vincenzo
- John Beverly

**"Everybody needs to serve somebody…"**
-Bob Dylan, 1979

**"…it is not in man that walketh to direct his steps."**
-Jeremiah 10:23
KJV Inspired by
God 647 BCE

# Table of Contents

# INTRODUCTION

For the sake of clarity, this book is written with the 'K.I.S.S.[1] concept in mind and has more than enough scriptural quotes to offend everyone, except seekers of truth.

Within the many debates between Christopher Hitchens and Dinesh D'Souza, Christopher stated, in an almost pleading way, "Why doesn't anyone just use scripture to debate me? I would have more respect for them." This came after quoting Jesus' words at John 14:6

*"...no one comes to the Father except through me."* **NASB**

Christopher was correct when he said, "No one knows the mind of God and should not presume to speak for Him." When religious leaders do not use the Bible in discussions and debates, man-made religion gets started and poisons everything.

---

[1] "Keep It Simple Stupid"

Man-made religion certainly poisoned Christopher, as well as others. In one of Christopher's last interviews before his untimely death, his friend, Richard Dawkins, presented him with an award, giving a most eloquent, wonderful, and precise tribute to Christopher Hitchens. Christopher could not say, as he does many times at the beginning of his debates, "Thank you for that terse introduction." No, Mr. Dawkins captured how most people felt, me included, about this great, intellectual and brilliant man.

In each of Christopher's debates, his antagonists debated Christopher on his own turf, using science, philosophy, secular church history and quoting as many books and authors as possible, using double-point scrabble words (sesquipedalian).

Using those tactics, all of the religious leaders failed miserably. Why? It is simple: Christopher did a splendid job at the podium describing these religions and their sanguinary history, while the well-educated, so-called Christian religious leaders stayed far away from quoting the Bible, preferring instead to say things like, "The Bible is filled with allegory, metaphor, and contradictions."

They basically turned their backs on the admonition given at 2nd Timothy 3:16,17 where we read,

*"All scripture is inspired of God and is beneficial for teaching, reproving, and setting things straight."* **NKJV**

To call oneself a Christian, one must be "Christ-like" following Jesus' example, using the Bible. When setting things straight, for example, Matthew 4:6 shows us each time Jesus answered saying, *"It is written"* (**NASB**) in this case quoting from the book of Deuteronomy.

Jesus also said at John 7:16-18,

*"I speak not my words but he that sent me... whoever speaks of his own originality is seeking his own glory."* **NIV**

You will see with my research of the Bible in Chapter 2; I believe 100% the Bible is the inspired word of God. I also believe 100% in the verses at 2 Timothy 3:16,17.

Why not let the Bible interpret itself instead of speaking for the Bible, and thereby "poisoning everything?"

In the Bible, there are over 31,000 thoughts from God. True, they are situated in a way to stay hidden from the pompous, self-important, grandiose religious leaders of our day. When viewing the debates, you will hear these men starting off a sentence with "I _think_ God does this"... "I _think_ God wants" or "I _think_ God..." This is the very reason why man-made "religion poisons everything" - because it is _man's_ thoughts and not _God's_.

Why should this be so important to you? Jesus gives a warning at Matthew 7:13,14 and right before this scripture, Jesus tells us what we need to do. He adds,

_"Broad and spacious is the road leading to destruction whereas cramped and narrow is the road leading to life, and few are the ones finding it."_ **NIV**

Pew report expresses 7 billion people are in the organized religions of the world, according to their report approximately 4.9 billion make up Christendom and Islam forum, hardly a cramped and narrow road.

It has been estimated millions of people lived at the time of the flood in Noah's day, and only eight survived. Before the flood came, what were men, women and their children doing wrong which warranted their being destroyed? In the Bible, Matthew 24:38,39 tells us

*"...they were doing the ordinary things of life, such as eating and drinking, men marrying, and women being given into marriage, and they took NO NOTE, and the flood waters came and swept them all away."* **REF**

God's not big on numbers, but He is big on *"worshipping in spirit and truth"* as written in John 4:24. **NIV**

Why not take your Bible out and follow along with me, looking up every scripture, even if it is already quoted? This book will give you a solid scriptural answer to the questions and accusations brought up by

Christopher in the debates. Christopher was brilliant against the religious leaders debating him, but as smart as he was, he was no match for God.

If you watch the debates, you might say Christopher used the Bible more than his opponents; however, the following pages will endeavor to rectify this oversight. Even if you have read the Bible cover-to-cover or if you will be viewing scripture for the first time, in the pages to follow, you will come away with a completely different understanding than what you have been taught by man-made religion.

Before you dismiss this way of thinking, turn to Chapter Four entitled: "Where Are the Dead? /You're Going Straight to Hell for That One!" See for yourself if this is what you were taught by man-made religion. Yes, grab your Bible. It's a challenge!

# Chapter 1

# List of YouTube Debates

My opinion on the late and sometimes great, but always brilliant, Mr. Hitchens was poisoned by the sanguinary history of religion, the way it has poisoned in our time and in years past, as he states, by "man-made rules and teachings." If you were fortunate enough to have heard any of Christopher's debates regarding his book, god is Not Great: How Religion Poisons Everything and really listen to how he defends his position, you would hear, albeit with great reluctance, a plea for biblical understanding.

However, very little from the Bible was ever quoted. Indeed, for whatever reason - because they did not know their Bible, or because they were guided by ego or "one-upmanship," - most of his antagonists at the podium quoted secular history, philosophy, and the empty words of men, rarely using scripture. The goal of this book is to rectify this injustice. Christopher, many times during his discussions and debates, quoted the King James version of the Bible as what he 'thought' to be Bible history. Unfortunately, it was not accurate Bible history.

Christopher gave many examples of what he thought would back his understanding of an unjust and an unloving god, with only, at best, a cursory understanding and knowledge of the Bible. Many times, in the discussions, Christopher's opinion, gathered from a foundation of false man-made teaching, went unchallenged by the religious leaders. He complained endlessly about many issues which included, but were not limited to:

1. How man has been on the planet for 100,000 years, with no intervention from God for 98,000 of those years.

2. Irreverently referring to the son of God as "gentle, meek, and mild," showing up after the 98,000 years have passed.

3. Taking issue with the Ten Commandments as if those were the only laws from God for the Israelites.

4. Pointing to the annihilation of the Amalekites as a justification to show God as unloving and cruel.

5. Adding to these dispersions Abraham's sacrifice of his son.

6. Lumping the ugly habits of false religion traditions, like cutting off the female clitoris with circumcision.

7. Challenging the prophecies in the Bible, saying the "game was fixed."

8. Trampling the integrity of God by saying God supposedly acknowledges some people's prayers, while disregarding others.

9. Failing to answer why God allows pain, suffering, and death.

10. Using the false teaching of the Hell doctrine to cast aspersions on the integrity of God.

11. Falsely teaching the Trinity
12. Putting his trust in earthly man and science, not the Bible.

Why *should* Christopher believe or trust in the Bible, when his religious antagonists did not use the Bible during the debates?

Christopher's mentor, Eric Arthur Blair (a.k.a. George Orwell) who attended boarding school at the early age of eight, like Christopher, came to a similar enlightenment. Mr. Blair had the habit of wetting his bed. Each night, he would pray to reverse this course. Each time when his prayer went unanswered, he was sent to the principal's office where he would receive a beating.

Christopher many times would say, as a young child, he truly enjoyed receiving a scripture every week in his school and researching that scripture in the King James Version of the Bible. Christopher at a young age was very fond of the KJV Bible and said so. Who took all the respect and love for the Bible and poisoned this young boy? Who is to blame for not nurturing in this boy his love for the Bible he had at first?

Christopher explained exactly who was to blame when being interviewed in a video with Tony Jones at the Festival of Dangerous Ideas (FODI).

When asked about his early educational life in religious school, Christopher quickly answered, "I know no other way of churning out an atheist, than with the teachings in a religious school."

While reading his book, viewing the discussions or listening to a pre-recorded radio broadcast, one couldn't help but be taken in by Christopher's charm and intellect. He seemed genuinely honest in his answers.

Just as I did, you will find yourself caring very much for this man, almost wishing Christopher hadn't experienced the poison of false religion so early in his life. On YouTube.com, the following debates and discussions are available. Here are just a few of them, Christopher Hitchens versus/and:

- Archbishop Widdicombe
- Frank Truek
- Dinesh D'Souza
- Timothy Jackson

- Dennis Prager
- David Wolpe
- Douglas Wilson
- Jay Richards
- Mark Danner
- Lee Strobel
- William Lane
- Tony Blair
- Larry Taunton
- David Berlinski
- John Haldane
- Anderson Cooper
- Jim Dennison
- Al Sharpton
- George Galloway
- Bill Mayer
- Richard Dawkins
- Tony Jones

You will enjoy these videos as much as I have. We are fortunate to have them available to us so we can watch and listen to Christopher Hitchens' thought-provoking ideas of deception.

In this book, we will explore more missed opportunities to use God's word, the Bible, to resoundly answer the list of objections in the debates and any additional questions from Christopher.

I'm purposely staying away from the historic detail of why "religion poisons everything," mainly because Christopher with his book and during the many discussions, recordings and videos, does a marvelous job with this subject himself.

All you need to do is look up the discussion you're interested in and listen to what Mr. Hitchens has to say. In many of the videos, an audience poll is taken before and after the debate; you may be surprised to learn the outcome.

# Chapter 2

# Why Not Use The Bible?

In all the debates and discussions there is a conspicuous absence of the use of scripture and Bible history from his antagonists. The religious leaders explained this omission by saying, "The Bible contradicts itself." ... "The Bible is filled with allegory." ... "It is filled with conjecture." ... "Its history can't be relied upon." I say, "Oh, really?" Perhaps this is what you, too, have come to know and feel about the Bible.

Just so we position ourselves on the right side here, what does the Son of God have to say? Does Jesus, God's Son, feel the same way as the religious leaders in the debates? Is this how Jesus perceives God's word? Perhaps the religious leaders would like to know?

Jesus said at John 17:17

*"... Your word is truth."* **KJV**

In addition, Jesus prefaced his answer by saying, *"It is written"* **NASB** (Luke 4:4), quoting scriptures from Deuteronomy.

Jesus also warned anyone who spoke on their own and did not use the Bible, saying

*"Whoever speaks in his own originality, he is seeking his own glory"* **(John 7:18 REF)**

Yes, Christopher was correct in chiding these religious leaders who wear religious garb, turning their neck collars around, wanting to be seen in public places, praying, and wanting to be called "Reverend," "Pastor," or "Rabbi". The Bible tells us at Matthew 23:6-12 "Don't be called 'Rabbi,'... 'Father,'... 'Leader,'... you have one Heavenly Father, you have one Teacher, Jesus Christ, and all of you are brothers..."

The Bible warns us at 2 Timothy 3:5,

*"From these, turn away,"* **(KJV)** or in another translation...

*"Have nothing to do with them."* **(NIV Study Bible)**

Also, a good admonition for all religious leaders found in the same chapter at verse 16 and 17,

*"All scripture is inspired of God and is beneficial for teaching, reproving, and setting things straight, disciplining in righteousness so the man of God will be completely equipped and ready for every good work."*

Unfortunately, none of Christopher's antagonists gave God's answers from the Bible.

Let's talk a little bit about the Bible for a better understanding. Let's see why you can fully trust and believe in the Bible, just like God's Son.

The Bible covers 6000 years of man's history and took over 1,600 years to write. It contains 66 harmonious smaller books, collectively referred to as "Bible." Although there were 40 individual inspired writers, nearly all of whom did not know one another, there is only one <u>true</u> author: God.

2Peter 1:21 reads,

*"For prophecy never had its origin in the will of man, but men spoke from God as they were carried along by the Holy Spirit"* (**NIV Study Bible**)

It is estimated that all or in part, the Bible has reached 90% of the world's population. It is translated into approximately 2,600 languages, with over a million

Bibles being distributed each week. This does not include the Bibles being read on the world wide web. All this in spite of the early church doing its best to stop you from having this book. As you start studying the Bible, it is quite easy to see why one may be discouraged and disregard Jesus' words to

*"keep knocking and the door will be opened to you"* **(Matthew 7:7) NASB**

or even worse, to push ahead on your own understanding. Take, for instance, Martin Luther who stopped at 95 incorrect man-made teachings.

Even though we are grateful for the "List of 95", Martin Luther needed to keep studying to make sure of all things 1st Thessalonians 5:21 reads to

*"make sure of all things, hold fast to what is true"* **(NJKV)**

as there are far more than a list of just 95 wrong teachings.

To help you in your understanding of how the Bible is written, I use the following analogy: Think, if you will, of the Bible as a very large jigsaw puzzle with over 31,000 pieces, each piece being one scripture.

If the Bible truly is the inspired word of God, as the book of 2nd Timothy points out, then all the pieces must fit. If, at first, a piece or scripture seems unfamiliar or does not fit, you don't throw it away – or worse, push ahead on your own. That's how man-made religion starts. Rather you set the piece aside until you have more of the puzzle field into the Bible picture.

What is the Bible picture? Paradise Lost to Paradise Regained: This is the picture of the Bible. Paradise Lost through one man, Adam, who was made perfect, but lost that perfection, then passed this imperfection on to all of his offspring:

*"When Adam sinned, sin entered the world. Adam's sin brought death, so death spread to everyone, for everyone sinned"* **(Romans 5:12) REF**

Paradise Regained through one man, Jesus, God's only begotten son, perfect in every way, leaving his position in the spiritual realm and coming to earth

*"Have this attitude in yourselves which was also in Christ Jesus, who, although He existed in the form of God, did not regard equality with God a thing to be grasped, but emptied Himself, taking the form of a bondservant, and being made in the likeness of men. Being found in appearance as a man, He humbled Himself by becoming obedient to the point of death, ..."* **(Philippians 2:5-70) NASB**

The Bible calls this "The Ransom." A perfect man for a perfect man = The Ransom. No offspring of Adam could buy back sin and death from the Earth. Christopher spoke about God not intervening for 98,000 years of human history. Yet the Bible tells us, "God made a way out from Adamic Death" 4,000 years before Jesus came to the earth with the first Bible prophecy found at Genesis

3:15. More will be explained in later chapters about this very first prophecy and also, The Ransom.

In Chapter 1 of this book, we have listed and enumerated 12 of Christopher's objections. In Christopher's complaint about prophecy (listed as #7), he gave examples of a couple of prophecies, in his own words, "could be fixed." Christopher said, "Jesus asked for a donkey to ride into Jerusalem, so he fulfilled that prophecy by himself," and "All his parents had to do was read to fulfill the prophecy where Jesus needed to be born." I think you get the picture. Were there any objections from religious leaders for these thoughts from Christopher? Sadly, the answer is 'No'.

One of the most striking things about this book, the Bible, which will greatly increase one's faith in it, is prophecy. Of all the prophecies which have come true, I would like to share two of them with you:

The Greek historian, Herodotus, in the fifth century BCE, confirmed the manner in which Babylon was overthrown. However, the prophet Isaiah, in 732 BCE (200 years earlier), put to pen the fall of Babylon along with the name of the person who would do the conquering, a man named "Cyrus" (Isaiah 44:27 through 45:3).

Babylon was built with the Euphrates River running around its high walls, and with its iron gates, it was thought to be impregnable. In just one day, Cyrus overturned the great city, Babylon, by diverting the waters of the Euphrates River and with his army, walked directly into Babylon. In addition, Isaiah 13:19,20 speaks to an infinite destruction. Babylon, which was once called "the political, religious, and cultural center of the ancient Orient," is now hot, flat, deserted, and dusty, according to the Smithsonian Magazine.

If my recollection is correct, Jesus had to fulfill 300 major and minor prophecies such as,

*"They divide my garments among them, and for my clothing they cast lots"* **(Psalms 22:18) NWT**

Like Roman guards gambling for his clothing, Jesus being sold for 30 pieces of silver

*"I said to them, "If it is good in your sight, give me my wages; but if not, never mind!" So they weighed out thirty shekels of silver as my wages"* **(Zech 11:21-13) NASB**

Here is another prophecy fulfilled you will enjoy (one of many which escaped Christopher's notice), found in the book of Daniel. This prophecy is called the "Seventy Weeks of Year Prophecy," which pinpointed The Messiah's arrival right before he turned 30 and started his ministry. The Israelites, with this prophecy found in Daniel, knew the time when the Messiah would come.

In fact, they were asking John the Baptist if he was *"The Promised One"* **(Luke 3:15)**.

## *"ALL Israelites knew."* **ASV**

In addition, the only genealogy from Adam to Jesus is found in the same Book of Luke, starting at verse 23 through 38. I will give you the overall information of the prophecy and you do the research on the scriptures. (By looking them up, you will be unraveling the mystery for yourselves. It's my hope you will enjoy this exercise and become more familiar with your Bible.)

Daniel lived more than 500 years before Jesus was born. God gave information to Daniel which would make it possible to pinpoint when Jesus would be anointed (Daniel 9:25). The Israelites were very familiar with one day being equivalent to one year in prophecy, and seven days in a week really referred to 7 *years*. Many years earlier, Numbers 14:34 sets the stage. Seven weeks plus 62 weeks made a total of 69 weeks, multiplied by the number of days, for a total of 485 days, or prophetically, 485 years. However, when does the countdown start?

Again, if we go back to Daniel 9:25, the Bible shows us the countdown starts when the word goes out to rebuild Jerusalem.

The Bible tells us at Nehemiah 2:1, 5-8, the word went out from King Artaxerxes in the 20th year of his reign, which was 455 BCE. Now, subtract 485 years above from the year 455 and you have 29 CE; coincidentally, the same time when Jesus was baptized and started his ministry. Israelites, along with their religious leaders, knew this prophecy and had the genealogy, but refused to believe Jesus was the Messiah.

There are many more prophecies you can look up and research on your own and I would encourage you to do just that: watch your faith build in the one, true author of the Bible. The following reference link is provided to help you find out more about the devastating odds of Biblical prophecies and their probabilities.

(https://y-jesus.com/what-are-the-odds/)

The Bible is not a science book brought to us to study the great works of God. No, we have all eternity to come know the mind of our Heavenly Father. The Bible was given to us by God for the end of this old system of things, so we may know true knowledge, and perhaps some may be spared in the day of His anger. Zephaniah 2:3 gives such hope when we read,

*"Seek God, all you meek ones of the earth, who observe his righteous decrees, seek righteousness, seek meekness and you will probably be concealed on the day of God's anger."*
**REF**

Coinciding with the scripture above, Revelation 7:9,13,14 tells us,

*"There is a great crowd of people...which come out of the great tribulation"* (**REF**)... and make it through the end of the system.

With the help of archaeology over the last 100 years, a wealth of information has been unearthed. Contracts, attorney documents, etc. have greatly increased the understanding of _Greek words and how they should be used_, so Bibles translated today are far more accurate.

Here is a good question: There are so many Bibles available today. Which ones would be the best to start a study? Fortunately, the decision has already been studied and made for you. Professor Jason David BeDuhn has given all of us a book with his findings: *"Truth in Translation."* I'm grateful for the early KJV Bible, however not in the same way as Christopher was, with his keen insight and knowledge of literature. We need to be more interested in an accurate translation, as it relates to our lives.

The KJV Bible, published in 1611, is riddled with many mistakes and spurious scriptures being added, difficult to understand, written in archaic English, let alone with God's personal name removed almost 7,000 times.

Christopher, a scholarly Englishman, could probably deal with archaic English, but I can't. Let's see how you do with the word "shambles."

The Bible reads, *"sold in the shambles"* found in the early KJV at 1st Corinthians 10:25.

Have you got a clue as to what it means? I didn't think so. "Shambles" in this case means "meat market." Also, when translating Greek, one adds the punctuation marks. For instance, a notable mistake is found in Luke 23:43 where the comma in the early KJV is added <u>before</u> the word "today" making Jesus not tell the truth. It states,

*" Today you will be with me in Paradise,"* NIV

remembering Jesus was actually in the grave for three days. By putting the comma <u>after</u> the word "today," the meaning is completely changed:

*"I tell you today, you will be with me in Paradise."* **NIV**

Neither Matthew - 18:11 or Mark 7:16, as well as the last eleven versus of Mark, are not found in earliest manuscripts. But one of the most famous, spurious scriptures found at John 8:1-11 added in the KJV is also found in false religious movies. Perhaps you know this scripture? It said something similar to Jesus writing in the dirt with a mob of men and women wanting to stone a woman to death nearby. Then Jesus interrupts and tells them, "The one who has no sin, let him cast the first stone." It may sound nice, but it's not true; again, not found in any of the earliest other manuscripts.

Here is a new thought for you: The Bible was written for our present time. Like Noah had a rectangular-shaped box to make it through the end of his system (or the world as they knew it), we, too, have a small rectangular book to know and make it through the end of our own system, though this time, it will not be by a flood. If you turn in the Bible to the book of Daniel and read the 12th chapter verse 4 and 9, you will read about Daniel asking to know what he was seeing in the visions given to him. Those visions would later correspond with the vision given to John on the Island of Patmos.

Yes,

*"Seal up the book till the time of the end."* **REF**

Jesus makes this clear with his words at John 17:3,

*"This means everlasting life: they're taking in knowledge of You, the only true God, and of his Son, Jesus Christ."* **REF**

At this point, it would be good to add the word "accurate" before the word "knowledge" and not the inaccuracies of man-made religion.

One of Christopher's antagonists, John Lennox, an affable man, a defender of faith, and a debater, also chose not to use the Bible in their discussions, just referencing a scripture occasionally.

Unfortunately, John's understanding of the Bible, although sincere, teaches something *different* than what the Bible teaches, no doubt brought about by man-made religion. John perpetuates the Trinity Doctrine, not found in the Bible. A case in point: John WRONGLY referred to Jesus Christ (on more than a few occasions) not as the son of God, but as God himself. 1 John 4:15 reads,

*"If anyone acknowledges that Jesus is the Son of God, God lives in him and he in God."* **NIV Study Bible**

Although Jesus reflects a perfect image of his Heavenly Father and God's love, Jesus in no way ever claimed to be the one, true God.

It is good for the reader to know how man-made religion gets started, in this case by putting words in Jesus' mouth and not letting him speak for himself. John

10:36 in the Christian Greek scriptures of the Bible, Jesus refers to himself simply as "God's son."

1 Peter 2:22 says,

"There is no deception found in Jesus. **NASB**

*So* why not allow Jesus to say what he means? When coming up out of the water after being baptized, a loud voice was heard from heaven:

"This is My beloved Son, in whom I am well pleased" **(Matthew 3:17) NASB**

In John 14:28 Jesus said,

"...I go to the Father, for the Father is greater than I." **NASB**

Was Jesus really saying he, himself, was equal to the true God? In Philippians 2:6, The Bible teaches,

*"who, although He existed in the form of God, did not regard equality with God a thing to be grasped after"* **NASB**

*"But I would have you know, ... the head of Christ is God"* **(1st Cor 11:3) NASB**

To protect this man-made doctrine of the Trinity, some religious leaders try and say 'the scriptures just quoted applied to Jesus when He was on earth. However, Jesus when Resurrected back to heaven resumed his equal status with God.' This is not what the Bible teaches, 1st Corinthians 15:28 makes it clear

*"When all things are subjected to Him, then the Son Himself also will be subjected to the One who subjected all things to Him, so that God may be all in all."* **ASV**

**John 20:17** *"...Go instead to my brothers and tell them, 'I am ascending to my Father and your Father, to my God and your God."* **NIV**

Because God's son, Jesus, humbled himself, came to earth, and died a horrible death, God has raised his son to a higher position than Jesus had before?

*"For this reason also, God highly exalted Him, and bestowed on Him the name which is above every name."* **(Philippians 2:9) NASB**

This can't be, as there is no higher position than God; Jesus can't be equal to God, nor would he ever claim to be. Mr. Lennox, although sincere, is sincerely wrong, much like all the Israelites who were left by Moses 40 days at the foot of Mount Horeb. The Israelites, fresh out of Egypt, had Aaron build a golden calf so they could worship their new God. Yes, they were also sincere, but sincerely wrong. God wanted to annihilate the Israelites and start over with the offspring of Moses. After all, it was a covenant with Abraham, not the Israelites, to bring the Promised Seed (Exodus 32).

In closing, there are enough scriptures in the Bible for anyone studying to have an "a-ha moment." If you are a person searching for truth or are a person who wants to find fault. One of Christopher's a-ha moments in the debates (which fell on deaf ears) was found in Matthew 27:52, where Christopher said, "Evidently the Resurrection was quite popular at that time, quoting the above scripture."

Yes, there are many scriptures you'll need to take the time and do additional research. Unlike Christopher, continue following God's Son's advice to keep knocking. This scripture, Matthew 27:52, does not conform to what the Bible teaches about a resurrection. There is no correlation with the ones who are asleep in the memorial tomb (God's memory).

The scripture above does not say they were brought back to life. The Greek word used in this scripture is "Ana'stasis" which means to "stand up."

In the cemeteries in Jerusalem, where the bodies were buried, most were above ground in vaults, chambers or sarcophagi. After Jesus died, a great earthquake occurred during which time stones were cracking, graves were opened and tossed about, along with the dead corpses – a shocking spectacle to say the least. This same phenomenon has happened in our day in Guatemala and Popayan, Columbia with each of their earthquakes, reported by the St. Petersburg Times and Time Magazine. During one of the interviews, a Red Cross worker told what they had seen. "I was stunned by the sight of corpses bursting from their tombs in the cemeteries."

The reports coming into Matthew about the above occurrence, would be expressed excitedly and forgo the word "embellished." Be that as it may, the resurrection of the dead is a very important subject and is a key ingredient to the hope found in the Bible for everyone.

There is much more on the resurrection found in Chapter Four of this book – details you'll surely want to know.

# Chapter 3

## Why Does Your God Allow

## Pain, Suffering and Death?

C hristopher Hitchens asked on several occasions, "Why does your God allow all of this pain, suffering and death?" In this chapter, you are encouraged to answer this question using your own Bible with scriptures which will be provided for you. Not only will this be a good exercise for you; we may spare cutting down a few trees.

When Christopher posed this question to religious leaders debating him, he never received an answer. Don't look to false, man-made religion for the correct answer, because it doesn't have the answers (and never will).

However, the Bible *does* give a sound answer as to why mankind has suffered pain and death for all these years.

Larry Taunton, one of Mr. Hitchens' friends, asked Christopher during a debate, "What is your biggest complaint against the teachings of Jesus Christ?" Christopher answered, "Jesus' teaching 'the taking away of sin'."

He continued with, "I could perhaps pay your debts; I could perhaps serve time for you in prison, maybe if you were really sweet to me, replace you at the gallows, like in the <u>Tale of Two Cities</u>. What I can't do is take away your sins. No, you are responsible for your own sins. This scapegoat mentality of absolving people of their sin is atrocious." Again, Christopher's thoughts would go unchallenged.

Christopher is correct: As a direct descendant of Adam, he could not do anything to absolve you of your sins. As Psalms 49:7,8 expresses,

*"None of them could ever redeem a brother or give a ransom for him, the price for their life is so precious that it is always beyond their reach."* **REF**

The very first man, Adam, was created perfect but was caught stealing from God. This act of disobedience brought sin and death into the world. Sin and death spread to all men through this one man. Romans 5:12 reads,

*"Therefore, just as sin entered the world through one man, and death through sin, and in this way, death came to all men, because all sinned."* **NJKV**

I liken this verse to a bread pan. If dropped, the pan will no longer be perfect, and one corner may now be smashed in. From that point on, all bread baked in this pan will be missing a corner; perfection lost. God's Law, found in the Bible at Deuteronomy 19, states, the law is "life for life,"(KJV) no more, no less.

Adam was made perfect and lost life, so it took a perfect man to buy back sin and death from the earth. Christopher, as good as he might be, could never fit that bill. Jesus was not a descendent from Adam. Jesus came down from heaven and his life-force by God was placed in the egg of Mary, guarded by God's Holy Spirit (Luke 1:35).

The Bible refers to Christ's death as a "Ransom Sacrifice" (NIV) for all mankind – those who already died and those in the future who would someday die – and all are covered with this one atonement.

The 613 laws, with its many blood sacrifices, condemned mankind and pointed to the Promised Seed for redemption. Jesus came to fulfill the laws, all 613 of them, and no descendants of Adam could do this...only a perfect man. Mat. 5:17 reads,

*"Do not think that I have come to abolish the Law or the Prophets; I have not come to abolish them but to fulfill them."*

NIV Colossians 1:14 reads,

*"By means of whom we have a ransom, the forgiveness of our sins."* **REF**

At this point, Jesus Christ, the Promised Seed, the Ransom, must be illuminated to understand the importance of this death. This is the crushing blow to the serpent's head and the fulfilling of the first prophecy in the Bible, Genesis chapter three, verse fifteen. This also corresponded to the lamb's blood over-the-door-post in Egypt which allowed death to pass over and an old Covenant to be done away with. On the same day, many years later, God's son established his new covenant with his followers. Luke 22:19,20 tells us to,

*"Keep doing this in remembrance of me."* **NKJV**

Yes, once a year the most important date in the history of mankind goes unnoticed by Christendom and man-made religion, basically ignoring Jesus' command and teaching their followers to celebrate the resurrection instead.

Please take the time to look up the following scriptures in your Bible which will verify the ransom sacrifice:

- Ephesians 1:7
- Matthew 20:28
- 1 Peter 1:18,19
- Romans 3:23-26
- Romans 5:6-8
- 1st Corinthians 1:30, 7:23

A perfect man for a perfect man = a ransom. And through this ransom, man is now able to deal directly with God, not having to go through a priest (or any other person) or having to sacrifice animals (or anything else) or as the Mormon Church teaches, baptizing for the dead.

Let's go back to Christopher quoting from John 14:6 in the introduction:

*"No one comes to the Father except through me."* **NIV**

Perhaps this is why so many prayers go unanswered; we need to acknowledge Jesus' ransom as the <u>only</u> way to his Father.

The following paragraph is dealing with the last 6,000 years of man's history as it conforms to the genealogy found in Luke 3:23-38. It follows the first prophecy of the Promised Seed in Genesis to our current day, and NOT the beginning of all creation, or earth, or the universe (not to be confused as we move forward).

These questions may come to mind: "Okay, but why so long? Why delay and incur all of this pain and death for 6,000 years? Why not cut it off right after Adam sinned 6,000 years ago? Wouldn't that have saved us all a lot of headaches?" These questions take us to the crux of the matter and the past 6,000 years of man's history.

Why so long? **Step 1**: We first need to understand God's time table. **Step 2**: What are the issues being resolved? **Step 3**: Are we the only ones involved in these issues?

Step 1 (and this by no means is meant to console you, but rather to help give a timetable for the past 6,000 years): 2 Peter 3:8 states,

*"However, do not let this escape your notice, beloved ones, that one day is with God as a thousand years, and a thousand years as one day."* **NIV**

This is why even though it took 930 years for Adam to die, he died in less than a thousand years as God said he would. Genesis 2:17 (paraphrased) states, "In the day you break this Law, you will die." The 6,000 years is only dealing with man's history and not the beginning of all creation, or earth, or the universe. It refers to what happened 6 days ago in Genesis, in the garden.

# Two Creations, Two Beginnings

The Bible teaches two creations, not one. The very first creation was in the spiritual realm where God dwells, and the second creation, in the physical realm made up of atoms where man dwells. This first creation, the Bible teaches, was God's only begotten son, Jesus, in the first chapter of John. (John 1:1) (Although the Bible refers to Jesus as god – small "g" – it's a title which means "mighty one."

The apostle Paul was also referred to as "god" in the Bible, with a small "g" at Acts 28:6. In addition, Satan is referred to as 'The god of this system of things" 2nd Cor 4:4.

*"For though there be that are called gods, whether in heaven or in earth, as there be gods many, and lords many"* **1st Cor 8:5 KJV**

In John, if you read chapter 1 verse 18, it will give you more understanding.

For the sake of argument, let's say a trillion years ago in our measure of time. The eternal God[2] of the Bible, existing outside of time, having no beginning and no end, all alone, decided to share life. (In the mid-1700s mathematicians in France had a difficult time with the concept of infinity. For help, Voltaire pointed out, all they needed to do, was look to the depth of men's stupidity)

The first life, and the only life, directly created by God, is His **Only Begotten** Son Jesus.

The Bible tells us Jesus is the only creature ever directly created by God, and all other creatures came into existence and were created by God's Son (Colossians 1:15, 17) NASB.

---

[2] Psalms 90:2, Psalms 90:4, Revelation 10:6, and 1st Timothy 1:17

He is the image of the invisible God, THE FIRSTBORN OF ALL CREATION. For by Him all things were created, both in the heavens and on earth, visible and invisible, whether thrones or dominions or rulers or authorities—all things have been created through Him and for Him.

The Bible says Jesus became his master worker.

"Then I was beside Him, as a master workman; And I was daily His delight, Rejoicing always before Him" **NASB (Proverbs 8:30)**

...and brought all other things into existence. However, only God gave them life, which was something Jesus could not do (Psalms 36:9). Life is only passed on by life.

47

The first creatures, brought forth by God's son, were also in the spiritual realm: millions of angels, seraphs, cherubs and messengers (Psalms 103:20 and Hebrews 12:22).

Many years later, the second creation was in the physical realm made up of atoms, not of spirit. Like the book of John, Genesis 1:1 also starts with,

*"In the beginning..."* **(KJV)**

which is the beginning of the physical creation.

The first beginning was God's son and a host of spiritual creatures making up the heavens, and in the second beginning was the Physical Realm. Adam was created perfect,

*" You have made him a little lower than the angels;"* **NASB (Hebrews 2:7)**

Then given God's attributes of love, justice, wisdom, power, and a conscience (Genesis Chapter 1). Life is only passed on by life.

When Adam was created, he was given a great vocabulary and spent much time with God in the garden, while He brought all the animals for Adam to observe and name. God had a cherub watch over Adam while Adam explored his new home. (Perhaps the cherub's purpose was to guard against accidentally breaking a natural law such as gravity?) Just as man tested everything he had created, so, too, did God have the right to test what He created.

When God placed Adam in the garden, he had an abundance of food and was asked by God not to eat from a certain tree in the middle of the garden. James 1:13, 14 shows we are drawn out by our own desires, and this angel, left to watch over Adam, started to covet the worship from Adam to God. This angel is now given the name, "Satan" meaning, "resistor," corresponding to the King of Tyre in Ezekiel 28:13. Other names include "father of the lie", "manslayer", and "devil" (which means "slanderer.")

Revelation 12:9 reads,

*"And the great dragon was thrown down, the serpent of old who is called the devil and Satan, who deceives the whole world; he was thrown down to the earth, and his angels were thrown down with him"* **NASB**

Yes, for the last 6 days, God has allowed a **precedent** to be set for all time. Drawn out by his own desires, this angel forsook his position and deceived Adam's wife and both Adam and his wife took what didn't belong to them. In this process of telling the very first lie, never challenging God's power but raising the questions of God's right to rule and whether man could govern himself, these questions were raised in front of the whole heavenly host of spirit creatures. In this process, this fallen angel also called God a "*liar.*"

Time was needed to answer these questions, and at the same time, work out God's original purpose – Paradise Regained with the offspring of Adam.

To better understand just what happened, the following analogy is offered: Let's suppose you own the fastest race horse in all the land. Up to this time, your horse has never lost a race.

One day, a well-known competitor approaches you in front of a great crowd of witnesses and claims he has a new horse that is much faster, and in a race, his horse can easily defeat yours. In his arrogant claim, he goes on to say you have not been telling truth about the speed of your horse, and in a race with his horse, your horse would lose, hands-down. Declining the challenge or eliminating this person and his horse would not be an option, as it would leave more questions in everyone's mind. No, you would need to set a race date and allow the race to run the course. This would thoroughly answer all claims raised.

God is not running this show and cannot be blamed for this mess. His adversaries and Man are to blame for the pain, suffering, and death for all these years. After the six days have ended, no one in the future will EVER question God's right to rule!

When Jesus was being tempted in the wilderness 40 days after his baptism, Satan offered all the governments of the Earth if Jesus would do a single act of worship. Satan said,

*"all the governments of the earth belong to him"* **(Luke 4:5,6,7) NASB**

1 John 5:19 says,

*"...the whole world is lying in the hands of the wicked one."* **NASB**

There is so much more on this subject. There could be another book written on this adversary alone. However, take heart! There is good news at Daniel 2:44:

*"In the time of those kings, the God of heaven will setup a kingdom that will never be destroyed, nor will it be left to*

*another people. It will crush all those kingdoms and bring*

*them to an end, but it will itself endure forever"* (**NIV Study Bible**)

This verse coincides with the prayer Jesus gave us at Matthew 6:9,10 when he taught us to pray for God's government or Kingdom to come to this earth.

*"... Your kingdom come, your will be done on earth as it*

*is in heaven..."* (**NIV Study Bible**)

Think about it: Why are we to pray for God's government to come and be set up on earth, if - as Christopher said - we are going to heaven or hell? Perhaps that is not what the Bible really teaches?

Maybe, just maybe, God has another purpose for you and the earth. Please turn to Isaiah 45:18 and read the scripture.

*"For this is what the Lord says – he who created the heavens, he is God; he who fashioned and made the earth, he founded it; he did not create it to be empty, but formed it to be inhabited – he says: I am the Lord, and there is no other..."* **(NIV Study Bible)**

What do you think? More will be added to your understanding in Chapter Four where we answer this question: Will we ever see Christopher Hitchens again?

# Chapter 4

# Where Are The Dead? / You're Going Straight to Hell For that One!

*"Dust you are and dust you will return..."*

- **Genesis 3:19 REF**

nother discussion between Christopher and a panel of three, on the subject of death, was entitled "Is there Life After Death?" During this debate, like many others, the room was filled with personal pontification and worldly knowledge, with very little from the Bible.

Before we get into what the Bible teaches about death, I would like to start with a simple concept: Death is the opposite of life, this is why Ecclesiastes 9:4 tells us, *"a live dog is better than a dead lion."*

On the subject of death, we can learn much from the book of John, and the account of Jesus' resurrection of his friend, Lazarus.

You will be moved by the scripture at John 11:35 where it says,

*"Jesus gave way to tears."*

Yes, Jesus was caught up in the emotional moment with the sisters of Lazarus, and Jesus started to weep.

Here is someone whom God has given the power to bring the dead back to life, yet still he felt great sorrow for his friend who had passed away in death. The Bible tells us Lazarus was dead four days. In that four-day period of time, he wasn't in hell and he wasn't in heaven – yet Christopher was taught in his religious school when death occurs, immediately that person will go to heaven or hell. Perhaps this teaching will now change to "You go straight to heaven or hell on the fifth day?" <u>No</u>. Jesus said Lazarus had "fallen asleep in death" (John 11:11) REF For clarity, Jesus also said in John 11:14

*"Lazarus has died."*

Apostle Paul speaks to brothers falling asleep in death at 1Corinthians 15:6. In Acts 7:60, when Stephen was being stoned to death by a crowd of people, as he died, he asked God to forgive them, and, the Bible says,

*"he fell asleep in death."*

A loving God wants you to know what happens when a loved one falls asleep in death, so God inspired Solomon to write at Ecclesiastes 9:5

*"for the living know that they will die, but as for the dead, they know nothing at all."* **NIV**

Solomon adds in verse 10,

*"whatever your hand finds to do, do it with all your might, for there is no work, nor planning, nor knowledge, nor wisdom, in the grave, where you are going."* **(NASB)**

Similarly, Psalms 146:4 tells us,

*"our spirit goes out, we return to the ground, on that very day our thoughts do perish."* **REF**

We are mortal and do not survive the death of our body; like a candle, when the flame is put out, it is gone. There is only one spirit from God given to man and animals alike, to animate our cells, and Ecclesiastes 3:19 tells us we all have the same eventuality, as one dies so the other.

# THE FIRST LIE:

## You positively will not die.

The very first lie told on earth is found in Genesis chapter three, verse four. This lie has been perpetuated by man-made, false religion for 6,000 years and teaches when you die, some part of you lives on and you immediately go to heaven or hell. This comes from a false teaching which concludes every person possesses a soul and this soul cannot die. However, this is not what the Bible teaches. Quite the contrary, the Bible teaches the soul dies. Ezekiel 18:4: *"the soul that sins will die"* (NIV) and again in verse 20:

*"The soul that sins will die."* **(NIV)**

Psalms 33:19 reads,

*"Deliver their souls from death"* **(REF)**

and also, in Psalms 116:8:

*"have delivered my soul from death."* **(REF)**

James 5:20: *"rescue my soul from death"* **(KJV, American Standard and the Reference Bible).**

The Bible teaches you don't have a soul, rather you ARE a soul: you are a living soul made up of three parts. In the first book of Genesis, God formed man out of the elements of the Earth, then animates the body with his active force or spirit, at the same time God breathed into his nostrils and Adam became a living soul. Take any one of the three away, body, breath, spirit, and you have a dead soul. No, the spirit is not you, rather it is God's active force or his holy spirit. In chapter one of Genesis, it says God's spirit was moving over the surface of the Earth.

Without being disrespectful, and for a lack of a better understanding in how to explain God's active force, it is a tool which God uses to get things done.

Jesus spoke of the Holy Spirit as a helper. He spoke of the helper as teaching, bearing witness, guiding, speaking, hearing and giving evidence. It is not unusual in scripture for something which is not a person to be personalized or personified. Wisdom is also personified at Matthew 11:19 and Luke 7:35, where it is depicted as having both *"works"* and *children."*

The apostle Paul personalized sin and death along with undeserved kindness as kings (Romans 5:14,17,21 and 6:12), Paul speaks of sin as,

*"receiving an inducement",* **(KJV)** *working out covetousness", "seducing" and "killing"* **(Romans 7:8-11)**,

yet it is obvious that Paul did not think sin was a person.

Not until the 4th century did false religion start teaching the Holy Spirit was part of a "godhead" and becoming official Church Dogma. Also, the Greek word for "spirit" was then translated as "ghost." Knowing the Trinity was not taught by early Christians, the translators took it upon themselves and inserted a spurious scripture at 1 John 5:7 which reads, "the father, the word, the Holy Ghost, these three are one." You are encouraged to do the research yourself.

# Hell

1 John 4:8 says

*"God is Love",*

but Christopher was taught by his man-made religion that God tortured bad people for eternity in hell.

Allow me to ask you a question: If I told you about a man that had a punishment for his unruly children by taking their hands and holding them over an open flame, would you really want to know this person? On the other side, if a religion got you to believe this about God and hell, that religion could really make some money – a <u>large</u> amount of money.

The word "hell" replaced the Hebrew word "Sheol" and the Greek word "Hai'des". The Hebrew word "Sheol" is the common grave of mankind, not a fiery place of torture. The archaic English word "hell" was used as a replacement for "Sheol" and at the time, the word meant "to put under the ground" as in "helling potatoes" (Colliers Encyclopedia 1986 Volume 12, page 28). (Vine's Expository Dictionary Old and New Testament Words, 1981 Volume 2, page 187). You are encouraged to do your own research.

Deuteronomy 32:4 calls God,

*"The Rock, perfect is his activities, all his ways are JUST."* **NASB**

Man-made religion will tell you, if a man is bad all his life (perhaps for 70 to 80 years), a just God will sentence that man to a fiery place of torture for eternity? I really don't think so. And it would be wise of you not to believe this man-made doctrine as well.

# Gehenna and the Lake of Fire

When did all of this start - about hell, a fiery place of torture - and where did it come from? None of this is even mentioned in the Hebrew and Aramaic scriptures (the first 39 books of the Bible, and the remaining 27 in Greek). However, here is what is mentioned and linked to the word "hell": Gehenna and the Lake of Fire. Both of these are found in the Christian Greek scriptures, and are used in connection. Let's learn about Gehenna first, and the valley of Hinnom.

The Greek word "Gehenna" appears 12 times in the Christian Greek scriptures and many translators took liberty to replace it with the word "Hell." The ancient tribes like the Canaanites, Ammonites and other tribes worshipped their false gods, "Baal", "Moleck", and others. In their worship, they would use human sacrifice, on or near the valley of Hinnom.

Complicit was Jezebel, a bad character in the Bible, and with her help working with other tribes, she induced the wicked kings of Israel (namely King Manasseh and others) to worship Baal and Moleck, including joining in on human sacrifice. How did the true God feel about this?

In your Bible, turn to Jeremiah 32:35. It reads, in part,

*"These detestable things would not even come into God's heart."* **REF**

(Does this sound like someone who would want you to be tortured in fire for eternity?) There was even a law punishable by death given to the Israelites if anyone were to worship these gods. Yet man-made religion, through its false teaching of hell and torture, has impugned the God of the Bible with this loathsome quality; teaching young Christopher this is what the God of the Bible will do to you as a punishment if you are bad. Oo-we! There is a day of reckoning coming. Don't be caught with those religious leaders who espouse the teachings of hell, as a fiery place of torture.

David Kimhi Jewish commentator 1160 1235 CE offered this explanation" He goes on to explain, the reason Gehenna was used by Jesus in illustration, is because Gehenna was a garbage dump in Jesus' time. Trash was burned and fires were kept burning where an occasional dead person was thrown, who was not thought worthy of a resurrection or a burial (criminals, for example.)

The lake of fire means the second death with no resurrection. None of these words are a fiery place of torture which the religious leaders of Christendom have twisted to their meaning, for so many years. "Man-made religion poisons everything."

Romans 6:23

"*For the wages of sin is death...*" **Not torture!**

# Christopher Asked, "What is Your Choice?"

Christopher said from what he was taught in his religious school, there were only two choices: heaven or hell. Is this what your church is teaching you? I ask because that's not what the Bible teaches.

God's original purpose for this earth, and mankind, was to have earth become a park-like paradise for all of Adam's offspring. In chapter two of Genesis, God put Adam in a park (which He, himself, had planted), and told Adam to be fruitful and fill the Earth and cultivate the garden (Genesis 2:15). Adam's work included being a steward and having all the animals, land, or sea, in subjection.

A couple more questions for you: Have you ever been to any of the National Parks, let's say like Yosemite National Park? When arriving through the west side tunnel, Christopher would say, it's a transcendent moment. The tunnel opens, looking over the whole valley in front of you. In that moment, you will be overwhelmed with what you see. It's as if God touched this valley with his finger, the beauty is so amazing.

Can you imagine the Garden of Eden, and what it would have looked like to Adam when he opened his eyes for the first time and saw the home God had provided for him?

Question Two: If Adam had never disobeyed God and taken from the tree, where would Adam be today, along with his offspring? God's purpose was not to have Adam's offspring to fill the heavens; they were already filled with millions of spirit creatures from the first creation.

Jesus Christ instructed his followers to pray for his Father's badly needed government to be extended to this earth. That is correct: The Bible teaches God's purpose is to have Adam's offspring here on earth in a park-like paradise. When one reads Psalms 37:11, we are told,

*"The meek will possess the Earth and find exquisite delight in the abundance of peace,"* **(REF)**

Psalms 37:29,

*"The righteous will possess the Earth; they will live forever on it."* **NIV**

## Two Resurrections

As there are two creations taught in the Bible, there are also two resurrections. (No, this is not referring to a resurrection of individual examples, as someone brought back to life for a short while, only to then die again.)

God, in His wisdom, knows His in-corruptible government we pray for to rule over the earth cannot be made up of non-humans. Angels would not fit the bill to make up this government, not having insight, not knowing the life, feelings, and the understanding that genetically make up humans. Even man can't govern man on his own; 6,000 years have proven this fact.

No, God's government needs to have humans who have spent time on this earth and have been tested in all respects, as to their loyalty, to their faith, all the way to death, not unlike their King.

Hebrew 4:15 says,

*"For we do not have a high priest who cannot sympathize with our weaknesses, but we have one who has been tested in all respects, but without sin."* **REF**

Hebrews 5:8 goes on to say,

*"Even though he was a son, he learned obedience from the things he suffered."* **NIV**

Humans make up a small number in God's government, and part of the first resurrection, must be "Christ-like" and demonstrate the fruitage of God's spirit. Galatians 5:22,23:

*"The Fruit of the Spirit is love, joy, peace, patience, kindness, goodness, faith, mildness, and self-control."* **NIV**

1 Corinthians 6:9,10 shows the hard fight they must put up to make change in their life, to take part and rule with Jesus in God's government (to be in this group you must make change in your life.)

These humans (both male and female) who have the opportunity to reign in heaven as Kings with Jesus, are adopted by God. They are, so to speak, hand-selected by God through the use of his Holy Spirit. The Bible reads in Ephesians 1:5,

*"For he foreordained us to be adopted as his own sons, through Jesus Christ according to his own good pleasure and will."* **NIV**

As we fit the pieces of the puzzle together, Jesus says, speaking to the ones who make up part of the government, John 10:16:

*"I have other sheep* NOT *of this fold, these too I must bring."* **REF**

For you to appreciate this, it will take much study on your part, as this is a sacred secret unfolding from the first prophecy about the Promised Seed. Without going into too much depth, a cursory understanding of the Temple in Solomon's time will set the stage. Briefly, you have the Most Holy Chamber, with the Ark of the Covenant representing God's throne and only one High Priest is allowed to have access. Then, you have the Inner Courtyard where only the Priestly class is allowed.

Lastly, you have the Outer Courtyard where citizens under this arrangement may station themselves.

All of this structure represents Heavenly Jerusalem, God's government that would soon be extended to the earth. Under the Priestly King Christ Jesus' rule, Daniel 2:44 informs us,

*"In the days of those kings, the God of Heaven will set up his kingdom, it will crush and put an end to all the kingdoms of the Earth, it itself will stand to time indefinite."*

All of this being supplied to you, a lot more study is needed. You have been given the outline, but now you need to fill in the full picture.

Although it is true the Bible refers to a small number of Adam's offspring who are a part of this new government, this does not apply to people who have lived and died before Jesus' resurrection to heaven.

No, the Bible makes it plain: Jesus is the first fruit; the first resurrected back to his life in heaven.

1 Corinthians 15:20:

*"But now Christ has been raised from the dead, the first fruits of those who have fallen asleep in death. Since death came through one man, resurrection of the dead comes through one man."* **NIV**

The Bible tells us John the Baptist will not go to heaven, as he died before Jesus was resurrected. Matthew 11:11 in part says,

*"No one born of women is greater than John the Baptist, yet the least one in heaven is greater than he."* **NIV**

The Bible teaches the vast majority of people who have lived here and died, both righteous and unrighteous, have the opportunity to be brought back, right here on Earth.

Christ has been given the power to resurrect the dead, told to us at John 5:28:

*"Do not marvel at this, the day and the hour is coming when all those in the memorial tombs will hear his voice and come out."*. **REF**

If you are one of the ones Jesus is speaking about, being in God's memory (the Memorial Tomb), you may very well be welcoming back the late Christopher Hitchens in the second resurrection, to a Paradise Earth

# Chapter 5

# Saddam Hussein and Family, Yes, The Amalekites, No

Hebrews 4:12 paraphrased reads,
"...*God's word is sharper than a two-edged sword... and is able to discern thoughts and intentions of the heart.*" **NIV**

Without the ability to copy Hebrews 4:12, Christopher changed his thinking after 9-11 and the attack in New York on the Twin Towers. He shifted thoughts, much to his friend's surprise, to being aggressive towards the war and Saddam Hussein and family. They were a very wicked family, no doubt, but no more so than the Amalekites.

Deuteronomy 9:5 reads,

*"It is not because of your righteousness or your integrity that you are going in to take possession of their land, but on account of wickedness of these nations, the Lord your God will drive them out before you, to accomplish what he swore to your fathers, to Abraham, Isaac and Jacob"* **(NIV Study Bible)**

Yet Christopher took the side of the Amalekites without any understanding of Bible history, and of course, from the online debates and discussions, no push-back from his antagonists.

God lovingly chose to work with the offspring of Adam – this being you and me. God was in his full right to put Adam and his wife to death 6 days ago in the garden and start over with a new creation, but then Christopher, you, and I would not be here. Within Adam, the whole human race that has ever lived on this earth was contained.

On a deeper level, Jesus, when taking a human form with a perfect body, carrying inside it an entirely new human race, although not used, bought all of us back with the delivery of his perfect human life to his Heavenly Father – again, a ransom fully paid.

To sum it up, God is working within a time frame, using imperfect humans, and an angelic adversary bent on stopping this Promised Seed from ever coming to earth. I believe out of 40 kings that ruled in Israel, only 4 were counted as "good." Now on top of this, God needs to intervene quite a few times for all to take place as it should. This intervention is to stop us from destroying ourselves, before God's time frame is complete. We wouldn't have made it this far if he hadn't intervened with the flood in Noah's day, or if he hadn't changed the language. Let's take a look in Genesis and see what God says before changing the language, in chapter 11, verse 6.

*"Look, there is nothing they can't accomplish with one language."* **NIV**

Intervention by God secured his timetable moving forward, if not, perhaps with one language, mankind would have blown itself up long ago?

As to the Amalekites, have you ever been working, trying to concentrate and had a mosquito, with its high-pitched sound, buzzing near your ear? If so, in no time, you just want to swat it away. This analogy pretty much sums up the history between God and the Amalekites. When the Israelites were leaving the wilderness after forty years, they needed to cross over other tribes' territories to get to the Promised Land.

However, out of politeness they would ask for permission before crossing. Yes, the first tribe was the Amalekites, used by Satan, without provocation to attack the Israelites. Joshua fought back and the Israelites were able to proceed (Exodus 17). The attacks from the Amalekites continued for 100 more years. Even King David was not immune, and his wife was kidnapped by

Amalekites. The Bible teaches us David took 400 men and was able to eventually rescue her.

Finally, the God of patience, with the ability to resurrect anyone He chooses, had enough and wanted the Amalekites to be completely wiped out. Unfortunately, the Israelites did not accomplish a complete elimination as descendants of the Amalekites reared their ugly heads again, this time in the book of Esther. The Bible describes a very wicked, Saddam Hussein-type of guy who is named

## *"Haman"* (Ester 3:1-11) KJV

Haman wanted to wipe out all the Israelites once again. No Christopher, it was the opposite. The Amalekites wanted to commit genocide on the Israelites and God, having all the abilities of discernment (found in Hebrews 4:12), had no choice but to stop the Amalekites.

# Chapter 6

# Isolating the Ten Commandments

hristopher, whether within the debates or outside of the debates, had great animosity towards the Ten Commandments. His bone of contention was neither he nor the Israelites, nor anyone else for that matter, needed the Ten Commandments in order to be civil. Christopher would say, "Do you think the Israelites were breaking all the laws of the Ten Commandments until they got to Mount Sinai to receive these laws? Preposterous!" From this he would then bring up the Golden Rule with pride because its origin is not from the Bible. However, he couldn't fully embrace the Golden Rule and gave an analogy of doing harm to Charles Manson before Charles Manson could do harm directly to him. And again, all of this thinking basically went unchallenged.

The thought process described above can be found in several of the debates. When I listen to Christopher's analogy on the Golden Rule, I can't help but cringe.

400 years earlier, before any laws or the Ten Commandments, in Genesis 39:9, a man named Joseph (his family was in line to the Promised Seed) refused the advancement of Potiphar's wife stating,

*"It would be unthinkable for me to do this against my God."*

**NIV**

Adam was made in God's image with love, justice, wisdom, power, and a conscience.

God had just saved the descendants of Abraham from slavery in Egypt and led them to Mount Horeb. This is counter to what Christopher said in the debates, referring to a dictatorship. God asked if the Israelites wanted him as their God. In Exodus 24:7, God gave this tribe 613 laws to follow – not just 10 – although the first 10 were written by Him. No descendants of Adam could ever follow these 613 laws completely, as you would have to be absolutely perfect to accomplish this.

So, God allowed certain members of this tribe to be priests and cover over their sins every year with blood sacrifice. The Law and these blood sacrifices pointed to the need for this Promised Seed (Matthew 5:17) to come to earth and fulfill the 613 laws for all the descendants of Adam.

Christopher, in the debates, looked strongly to science for his refuge, certainly not the Bible. Without a knowledgeable understanding of the 613 laws given to the Israelites from God, Christopher isolated the Ten Commandments as if this were the complete list, without being called to account.

It is true, God did not give us the Bible to understand His great works, but gave the Bible to us to understand why we find ourselves in this state of affairs, and to best guide humanity through this ungodly system we find ourselves in. However, Christopher, without knowledge of what the Bible really teaches, constantly pointed at the 10 commandments without substance, disregarding the other 603 laws, and thus was free to say what he wanted without rebuttal from the so-called religious leaders debating him.

While we are on the subject of the 613 laws, allow the Bible to clear up other things Christopher had to say. Not knowing about the history and the purpose of the 613 laws, Christopher spoke harshly about this God, pointing to him as a dictator.

First, it's no easy task to deal with the Israelites over a 4,000-year time frame, to bring us the prophecy of the Promised Seed, and they were uncooperative to say the least (Deuteronomy 9:6.)

God needed the Israelites to be clean and keep their immune system up, as they were getting further away from Adam and perfection, so quite a few laws were based on this alone. 3,500 years after the 613 laws were given, a doctor named Ignaz Semmelweis tried to introduce washing ones' hands thoroughly before doing another procedure in a hospital, especially after coming in contact with a cadaver.

The Scientific Community drummed him out of medicine. Yet in the Bible, according to Numbers chapter

19, any person coming in contact with a dead animal or human must take a bath and wash thoroughly, along with the washing of their clothes. Also, Leviticus 13:1-5 discusses how the Israelites must quarantine the sick.

Deuteronomy 23:13,14 instructs the Israelites when nature calls, they must take a tent stake with them out of the camp, dig a hole and cover afterwards. In addition, the Israelites were not to draw water or go near water which had something dead floating in it, this is no easy task.

Imagine this, if you will: the Israelites marching in the wilderness, hot and thirsty, coming to a pond of water. Seeing another tribe of children playing and splashing around while the women of the same tribe would be filling their earthenware jars with water for drinking. Some distance away, a bloated, dead carcass of an animal is floating in the pond.

With the new law, the Israelites would have to move on. Approximately 3100 years before the microscope was invented, these laws were given to the Israelites. If not God, how would this early tribe know to do these things?

Christopher complained about not being able to eat ham as part of the "dictator conspiracy." True, God in his 613 laws didn't take the time to supply different recipes on how to cook certain foods, so as not to make one sick.

In brevity, God stated the animals and sea creatures not to be eaten. (I can imagine Christopher at this point in a Japanese restaurant, enjoying eating a poisonous blowfish, condemning God in every bite.) Christopher also spoke about the "Flat Earth Society" when all they had to do was read Isaiah 40:22, to know

*"the Earth is a circle or sphere",* and Job 26:7, to know

the earth *"hangs upon nothing."*

Ecclesiastes 1:7 speaks ecologically about how water is drawn from the ocean to replenish our rivers and then returns to the ocean to start the cycle again. In many discussions, Christopher gave an analogy about an aborigine finding a ticking, gold watch on the beach. The aborigine knows it's not a rock. At this point, as an evolutionist, Christopher would have you believe the gold watch got there not by a maker, but by evolution[3]... the gold watch found by the aborigine was in hundreds of intricate pieces placed in a shoebox 14 billion years earlier by no one. Then, shaken for the 14 billion years and presto! Something as complicated as a gold watch miraculously evolved from the pieces to be found by the aborigine.

In response to that suggestion, I will use the words Christopher often said in the debates, after explaining something taught by religion: "No, thank you. I don't want it, I won't have it, keep it to yourself."

Let's finish with the Golden Rule and just add Jesus made the Golden Rule more positive. In Matthew 7:12, Jesus tells Christians

*"to DO to others as you would like them to do to you."* **NIV**

Christopher spoke about Jesus' story of the Good Samaritan, quick to point out he was neither a Jew nor a Christian, but did a good deed. The Samaritan followed Jesus' new twist on the Golden Rule by treating the

---

3 PHD Steven Meyer's book Darwin's Doubt

injured man as he himself wanted to be treated (Luke 10: 25-35).

Christopher would not credit Christendom when a person inside of religions does great humanitarian things for his fellow man. And I'm sorry, but in most cases I have to agree with Christopher and add these people act "Christ-like" and do these good things sometimes in spite of that person's religion and their teachings.

A person who follows in the steps of the Good Samaritan and the new Golden Rule (*here is where Christopher and I part*) demonstrates a strong conscience and a loving heart, a gift of the Holy Spirit given to them by their Creator, not by man-made religion.

# Chapter 7

# Jesus: Gentle, Meek & Mild

In many debates, Christopher referred to Jesus irreverently as "gentle, meek, and mild." Christopher was strong when dealing with his opponents, but in comparison to Jesus, he was somewhat of a milquetoast.

It's easy to see why Christopher might have formed such an opinion at an early age, as man-made religion portrays Jesus as a pusillanimous weakling in its portraits and statues.

Quite the contrary, Jesus was no weakling. Jesus was born a perfect man and was <u>not</u> a descendant of Adam. The first time we learn about Jesus' boldness is when he is 12 years of age, found by his 'foster' parents after three days - 72 hours - in the temple speaking in the middle of a group of the most learned men of the time (Luke 2:42) No doubt they are trying to trap the young Jesus with questions about the many man-made traditions, but they did not. The Bible reports ALL of the men were astonished by his answers.

A little later, learning to be a carpenter at a young age - namely going into the forest, cutting the tree down, hauling the tree back to a workshop and forming furniture out of it – this was certainly no work for a weakling.

In Jesus' ministry, he braided a whip and went into the temple courtyard and overturned the tables of the money changers, whipping their animals outside of the courtyard, and not one of them stood up to him. The Bible tells us he did this twice,

*"And Jesus entered the temple and drove out all who sold and bought in the temple, and he overturned the tables of the money-changers and the seats of those who sold pigeons. He said to them, "It is written, 'My house shall be*

*called a house of prayer,' but you make it a den of robbers.'*

**Matthew 22:12 & 13 ESV**

*And making a whip of cords, he drove them all out of the temple, with the sheep and oxen. And he poured out the coins of the money-changers and overturned their tables.*

**John 2:15 ESV**

Jesus had no fear when it came to his preaching the kingdom good news, and if religious leaders got in the way, he would tell them to their faces what he thought of them. Read Matthew chapter 22,23. Jesus would say, knowing their wickedness, the following:

- Hypocrites
- Blind guides
- Fools
- Blind ones
- Serpents

- Offspring of vipers
- Killer of the prophets and more.

As you study your Bible, you will definitely form a different opinion than Christopher or man-made religion.

When you watch the debates, it's sad knowing what the Bible teaches about the certain subjects Christopher is complaining about, when none of his opponents give a satisfying answer to him from the Bible. "Man-made religion poisons everything."

# Chapter 8

# The Sacrifice of Abraham's Son

**M**any times in the debates Christopher complained about Abraham being asked to kill his son: "What kind of a God would ask such a thing?" In some of the debates, he would say (without any rebuttal) "This is crazy. I could never do anything like this, let alone worship a God who would ask me to do this." Again, this statement – like so many others – would go unchallenged.

The first prophecy in Genesis chapter 3:15 speaks about *a seed which would bring a crushing blow to the serpent's head.* After a long time, nothing is said about the seed, until approximately 2,018 BCE. Abraham was born 352 years after Noah, the 10th generation from

Noah through his son, Sham. Abraham was not the first-born son (he was born 60 years after his brother). However, he was treated as firstborn by his father because of his faithfulness and love for God. The Bible says Abraham became God's friend and it was through this friendship God would bring his Promised Seed. Yes, from the offspring of Abraham as stated in Genesis 22:18.

This was unique because the wife of Abraham, although still beautiful, the Bible tells us, was far past the childbearing age. When Sarah, Abraham's wife, heard this news somewhere around the age of 91, she laughed, and later chose to name their son "Isaac" which means "laughter." With all the time Abraham spent with God, his relationship with God grew more intimate and his faith grew stronger.

Over the age of 100 years, Abraham loved his son, Isaac. Even though God asked Abraham to sacrifice Isaac, He had no real intention of allowing Abraham to go through with this test. Abraham knew everything would be okay. Please read Genesis Chapter 17. Abraham tells his manservant he is taking his son over there to worship and *they would return.* Abraham already had God's promises Isaac would be blessed and would bring forth a nation.

So now we need to contemplate what this whole thing was really about. Why did God put His friend through this horrible drama? Abraham loved his son dearly, just as much as Christopher loved his children, or you and I love our own children. Why? This drama is to show each one of us what the "greater Abraham" (Yahweh) was about to do two days (in His time) from then, with His "only begotten son" (Jesus, the Promised Seed).

Every parent should feel stabbed in the heart when they think about this drama and the gift God has given us. The Bible is not for Christopher or his close friends (who are sometimes referred to as the four Headless Horsemen - Headless Horsemen because they can't bring themselves to believe in a simple statement found in Hebrews 3:4:

*For every house is built by someone; but He who built all things is God"* KJV

They preferred to believe life was passed on by nothing, or as one of them said when pressed in an interview, "maybe aliens from another world".

The Bible is not meant for the well-educated religious leaders of our day; they are all too smart for the Bible. The Bible is a spiritual gift given only to a few who reach for it and really want to know its truth. And it's a privilege! Jesus prayed to his father and thanked him for giving the Bible to us the way it is written. Luke 10:21 states:

*"...I publicly praise you father, Lord of Heaven and Earth, because you have carefully hidden these things from the wise and intellectual ones..."* **NIV**

## Circumcision

In the same breath as the above thoughts, Christopher also claimed God hurt children with genital mutilation, lumping removing the female clitoris, by worshipers of false gods, with circumcision. Not even close, Christopher! So, let's take the removal of the female clitoris and put that act on its own.

At this point, it may be good to know, at Jesus' death, along with taking away 611 laws of the 613 given to the Israelites, his death also removed the Abrahamic Covenant of circumcision and the Sabbath. Unfortunately, this triggered the scripture where Jesus says,

*"I came to put a sword between them"* in Matthew 10: 34. **NIV**

The true meaning behind this scripture, Jesus knew how deeply ingrained the Israelites had the law and circumcision inculcated in their hearts and minds. No, it wouldn't be easy to let go. In fact, the controversy over circumcision was argued by early Christians for close to 30 years before its acceptance.

It was exceedingly difficult for the Israelites to understand and except 1 Corinthians 7:19 which relates,

*"Circumcision means nothing and un-circumcision means nothing, what means something is observing God's commandments."* **NIV**

The new Jerusalem is a heavenly Jerusalem not an earthly Jerusalem. There is no need for religions to be fighting over a strip of land. Hebrews 12:22 reads:

*"But you have approached, a Mount Zion and the City of the Living God, Heavenly Jerusalem."* **NIV**

Circumcision is by spirit, a circumcision of the heart. Romans 2:29 shows the first Christians,

*"He is a Jew that is one on the inside and his circumcision is one of the heart by spirit not by written code, that person's praise comes from God, not by people."* **ASV**

Again, all of the laws, all of the blood sacrifices and circumcision and the Sabbath, were fulfilled in God's son and it's through Jesus' ransom there is a new covenant established.

Hebrews 9:15 reads, when speaking about Jesus,

*"That is why he is a mediator of a new covenant in order that because a death has occurred for their release by Ransom from the transgressions of the former Covenant, those that have been called may receive the promise for an everlasting inheritance."* **REF**

This book has endeavored to simplify this very deep subject found in the Bible, which takes far more study and coincides with information found in Chapter Three and Four of this book. But we are dealing with Christopher pointing his fingers at the early covenant and blaming God for this horrible mutilation. Unfortunately for Christopher he was wrong once again. This practice of circumcision is a mark of cleanliness and after making the covenant with Abraham, this mark of cleanliness was established. God told the Israelites to have this done to all male babies on the eighth day and this included breaking the rule of the Sabbath.

Understand, if the covenant is going to be broken, it must be for a vital reason. In fact, it must be for something unrecoverable if missed; in other words, 'perishable' event. Circumcision fits this unique requirement exactly. It turns out circumcision must be performed on the 8th day for good reason. Modern research demonstrates vitamin K causing blood coagulation is at its highest percentage at 110% on the 8th day after birth. Isaiah 55:9 tells us,

*"As the heavens are higher than the Earth, my ways are higher than your ways and my thoughts are higher than your thoughts."* **REF**

Through the ransom paid, we have eternity to understand why all of this was put in place. We will end with after Adam sinned against God, man was no longer able to have the same relationship. With man sinful, God put things in place so He could deal with us and bring the Promised Seed.

# Chapter 9

# Christopher's Book: "god is Not Great"

Christopher's love for the early King James Version of the Bible puts him at a significant disadvantage as compared to the use of new, up-to-date reliable translations. Even the committee of the KJV Bible Society has updated one of their versions of the King James Bible: The Divine Name Edition King James Version of the Bible 400-Year Anniversary. The "better-late-than-never-edition". It is very good if you are reading and studying the bible. Even better, if you have an up-to-date and reliable translation with God's name included as He originally intended. (or as He originally gave it).

In chapter 9 of Christopher's book, _god is Not Great_, Mr. Hitchens talks about God's name "Yahweh" or "Jehovah" with very little background knowledge. Most people do not realize the word 'God' or 'Lord' are titles. "God" or "Eloim" means "mighty one" and "Lord" or "Adhonia" means "master."

God has a personal name which distinguishes him from all others. The disguised angel of light, opposer of Yahweh, Satan, has done everything in his power to keep His personal name from you. 2 Corinthians 4:4 reads,

_"Among whom the god of this system has blinded the minds of the unbelievers, so that the illumination of the glorious good news about the Christ, who is the image of God, might not shine through."_ **REF**

Yahweh or Jehovah meaning: "He that causes to become" first being the Hebrew "YHWH" translation and the later being the Latin "JHVH" translation of the Hebrew tetragrammaton for God's name, is found in the oldest manuscripts of the Bible a little under 7,000 times. This means God inspired the forty individual Bible writers to insert the four consonants, equaling the tetragrammaton almost 7,000 times - double what He is referred to everywhere else in the Bible (i.e., Sovereign Lord, Almighty God, Ancient of Days, God, Lord, and many others).

It is this author's opinion the removal of God's name from the first 39 books of the Bible as God intended to be there, has a profound effect on the reader. This removal of His name obscures clarity and blurs the line or division between Yahweh and the arrival of the promised seed. With Yahweh in place as He intended, it would be easier for the reader to accept Jesus as God's Son; not God.

The early King James Version of the Bible has taken out the name and replaced it with LORD and GOD in caps everywhere the tetragrammaton was found except four places. The most common place God's name is found, in the KJV, is Psalms 83:18

*"So men may know the name Jehovah is the most high over all the earth."*

Also, in part, the name is found in the word Hallelujah or Praise-Jah short for "Jehovah." The reason it is Jehovah and not Yahweh, is we use in English the Latin translation JHVH and not the Hebrew YHWH, just as we do with the name Jesus, not the Hebrew name Ye•shu•a.

I'm sure Christopher would be happy to know his favorite Bible with help from the KJV Society has rectified this oversight and now printed a new KJV with the Latin tetragrammaton replaced almost 7,000 times. It makes one wonder, why God's name was removed in the first place. Besides Satan, God's opposer, working his hardest to stop you from knowing God's true name, it goes back 200 years before Jesus came on the scene, starting with superstition and religious leaders, and then later after the death of the apostles when religious leaders once again removed the name. See if this makes sense to you: Over 1,600 years, God inspired forty different men to write His name just under 7,000 times, so a few people could then *remove* His name and replace the name with a title LORD or GOD in caps? Somehow it doesn't make sense when the same people allowed all the names of false gods to *stay* in the Bible (i.e. Baal, Moleck, Zeus, Hermes, etc.)

Let's see how Jesus felt about using Yahweh's name. When asked by his disciples how to pray, at Luke 11:1,2,

*"...Jesus was in a certain place praying and when he stopped,*

*one of his disciples approached him*

*and asked: Lord, teach us how to pray... So he said to*

*them, 'whenever you pray then, say: Father, let your name be*

*sanctified."* **REF**


Also, found in Matthew 6:9, Jesus teaches everyone the most important and first part of prayer. In chapter two of this book, you would have learned about the Bible picture to help you fit pieces of the puzzle into place.

Now we will be learning the theme of the Bible, that is, the sanctification of God's Holy name.

Jesus came to restore the value of the name "Yahweh" or "Jehovah", the Holy name for His Heavenly Father. Yahweh **or** Jehovah; it doesn't matter which name you use, just as long as you do. Today, the most popular use around the world is "Jehovah".

God has been called a liar and His personal name has been shoved aside by false religious leaders, hidden from man and trampled on for over 200 years.

Now 29CE, the Messiah is here, and Jesus is going to make a change. In Mark 7:6-8 Jesus tells the religious leaders,

*"...hypocrites...they keep teaching commands of men as doctrines, you let go of The Commandments of God and cling to the traditions of men."* **NIV**

This change is one of the big reasons the religious leaders of his time wanted to put Jesus to death. Jesus was using God's name in his ministry and teaching the truth, breaking away from their man-made traditions and false religious rules. Jesus, when teaching at John 17:26, will say,

*"I have made your name known and will continue to make known."* **REF**

Jesus knew how important it was to know and use God's name. Peter, in Acts 2:21, quoting from Joel 2:32:

*"All those who call on the name of Yahweh will be saved."* **REF**

All people of the earth have a personal name; if you want a friendship with anyone, knowing their name is step number one! The Bible tells us by Peter at Acts 15:14:

*"...God is taking out of all nations a people for his name."* **NIV**

There was a great light in the world at the time when Jesus and his apostles were on the earth. However, Jesus taught us through his parable of the wheat and the weeds, after he and his apostles were gone, the light would fade, Matthew 13: 24-30, 37-43. In Acts 20:29,30 Paul remarked after he was gone, wolves would come in amongst the Christian and "*Teach Twisted Things.*" After the death of the apostles, about a hundred years, apostasy blossomed and produced the churches of Christendom.

Far from proving to be a people for the Yahweh name, Christendom took God's name out of the Bibles, and added back Martin Luther's list of 95 and their teachings: adopting Pagan rituals, starting their Holy Wars, teaching dogma and acting immoral. Yes, as Christopher would say, "man-made religion poisons everything."

## How to Identify False Religion

*"There is a way which seems right to a man,*

*But its end is the way of death."* **Proverbs 14:12 NASB**

Hogwash, Horsefeathers, and Balderdash! How did all the nonsense get into Christendom? What nonsense is this book referring to, an evergreen tree coming back each year, Easter, colored eggs, rabbits, 3 Wiseman, a star to lead them, celebrating Christ's birthday and more.

Approximately 2,400 years before the promise seed arrived a man named Nimrod was born, son of Cush, son of Ham, son of Noah, Genesis 10: 6, 7, 8. Nimrod (the name means rebel), against God's wishes, congregated people together in cities which he ruled over. Setting himself up as a king/god over the different cities, 11 in all, including cities in Assyria.

Starting the Babylonian Empire with the city of Babel, along with himself, wife, and son as a trinity, many other false gods and goddesses where worshiped. However, after the language was confused, which caused people to spread out over the earth as God intended, they took with them all the false teachings. Later when the Roman Empire was being built, all the false teachings came back together, including many Triune deities.

The first Mother and Son worship was Tammuz an Ishtar from earlier Babylon. When Tammuz died a clump of his blood landed on a tree stump and an evergreen tree would come back each year. Women of the time would weep for Tammuz and wear a T around their necks.

Ezekiel 8:14

*"Then He brought me to the entrance of the gate of the LORD'S house which was toward the north; and behold, women were sitting there weeping for Tammuz."* **NASB**

as to the T worn around the woman's neck 2nd Corinthians 5:7 reads

*"We are walking by faith not by sight"* **ASV**

Two hundred years after the death of the apostles, about 314 CE is the time when secular history of Rome and all its false worship merged with the church under

Constantine. One thought was, let's make it easy for the Romans who are worshiping the "sun god" or saturnalia, to switch their drunken parties, too Christianity, now celebrating the birthday of the "Son of God".

To help with trimming this birthday celebration let's bring in the tree of Tammuz, decorating it with a star on top, one like the star that guided the three Magi, Astrologers, Wise Men, (condemned in both Leviticus and Deuteronomy) bringing gifts to the baby Jesus in the manger, found in most nativity scenes. No... sorry, read Matthew chapter two, the star led the astrologers to King Herod who wanted to kill Jesus. Also, there is no mention of how many Magi there are, only three types of gifts.

It was customary to bring gifts to a newborn king in some cultures, however early Christians never celebrated Jesus birthday. The astrologers found Jesus living in a house close to the age of two years old, not a baby in a Manger. God sends angels, not a star to notify shepherds in the field, about the new-born King. Much too cold to have sheep outside at night in December.

As for all other things linked to celebrating Jesus including the sun rise service, Easter, from the Anglo-

Saxon goddesses of spring and fertility, Eostre/Ostara. Keep in mind a reminder found at John 4:24

*"worship God in spirit and Truth"* **2nd Corinthians 6:14 NASB**

*"Do not be bound together with unbelievers; for what partnership have righteousness and lawlessness, or what fellowship has light with darkness?"* **NASB**

*"You adulteresses, do you not know that friendship with the world is hostility toward God?"* **James 4:4 NIV**

Apostle Paul, writing to the Galatians congregation, in chapter 1:8,9 tells us plainly how to identify false religion. Paul said,

*"Even if HE, or an ANGEL, were to teach anything different from what you have been taught let him be ACCURSED."* **REF**

This refers to the entire body of scripture, all 66 books. Paul's warning would include the angel, Gabriel, and Muslim teachings 600 CE, along with the angel, Moroni, and the Mormon church 1200 years after the Muslim teachings. Paul's words go further to include all the churches of Christendom and their teachings.

Here are a few false teachings perhaps they haven't thought about in times past: the false teaching by the Catholic Church forbidding priests and nuns to marry. Keep in mind the Catholic Church asserts Peter as being the first Pope, yet he was married and had a family!

Paul's letter to Timothy at 1st Timothy 3:2 & 4 in the United States Conference of Catholic Bishops Bible reads:

*Therefore, a bishop must be irreproachable, married only once, temperate, self-controlled, decent, hospitable, able to teach." "He must manage his own household well, keeping his children under control with perfect dignity."*

Ask yourself how many children would have been spared from the disgusting things perpetrated by priests and nuns, if the Catholic Church would have followed Paul's advice?

Another false teaching is a call to go to war in the name of God. No Christian in any country should ever go to war if he is a true follower of Jesus Christ.

*"They are not of the world, even as I am not of the world."* **John 17:16 KJV**

In John 18:36, Jesus answered the Roman Governor, Pilate,

*"Jesus answered, "My kingdom is not of this world. If My kingdom were of this world, then My servants would be*

*fighting so that I would not be handed over to the Jews; but as it is, My kingdom is not of this realm."* **KJV**

How many children from Christian parents would have been spared and not have been sacrificed to the gods of patriotism in all the so-called Christian countries which participated in World War 1? All-in-all, twenty-eight countries participated in that war, claiming to be Christian and have God on their side. To quote Abraham Lincoln, *"It would be far better if they were on the side of God"*

In the discussions and debates, Christopher pointed out (and rightly so), the word "Christendom" is not used after World War 1, perhaps due to embarrassment?

Consider this analogy: As a citizen of the United States, you decide to live and work in Paris for a few years. While in Paris, you're subject to Parisian law. You pay their taxes; you obey their traffic laws.

However, you would draw a line, as a US citizen, if France asked you to pledge your allegiance to their government, or go to war for them, you would remain neutral. Now being a Christian, or being Christ-like, you pray for God's government, show God through your conduct you want to be a citizen of his rule and government. As Jesus said, you pay back God's things to God (Mark 12:17). Jesus said you would be able to identify his followers by the love they had among themselves. (John 13:34-35) Christians or Christ-like, all would be brothers in any country they found themselves in, and would certainly not go to war.

If you need help with this thought, read Smedley Butler's book <u>War is a Racket</u> coming from the most decorated Marine before WW1.

Remembering the second greatest commandment is, from the words of Jesus,

*"to love your neighbor,"* **(Mark 12:31) NASB**

and the first,

*"to love God with your whole heart, mind, and soul."*
**(Mark 12:30) NASB**

Jesus, telling Peter to put his weapon away, in the garden of Gethsemane would have the same admonition for all Christians today.

False religion blessing the guns of soldiers about to go into battle, on both sides, brings to mind Christopher's words, "man-made religion poisons everything."

Google this documentary: "The real history of the Roman Catholic Church" this documentary shows how the weeds were sown into Christendom after Jesus and the apostles were gone.

Do these churches really demonstrate the fruitage of God's spirit found in the book of Galatians 5: 22,23?

# Chapter 10

# Christopher's Challenge

In most debates, Christopher made the following challenge: "Tell me something moral or Christian that I, as an atheist, can't do?" Not waiting for an answer, Christopher would go on to say, "Now think of something horrible that only a person in a religion would do?" Again, not waiting for an answer, he would then add, "See? You have already thought of one."

To answer Christopher's first challenge, when he asked for something a moral Christian could do that, he, as an atheist, couldn't do, I believe it would fall under Jesus' first and greatest commandment:

*"To love God with your whole heart, mind, and soul."*

**(Mark 12:30) NASB**

After listening to the debates and going over his book, _god is Not Great_ thoroughly, I don't see how Christopher would have been able to accomplish what Jesus asked.

Later, when reviewing a debate with William Craig and Christopher, Mr. Craig stated the very same answer, yet Christopher refused to acknowledge William with a response.

# Christopher Declares "Faith is Blind"

Again in the debate with Dinesh D'Souza both Dinesh and Christopher are asked a question about faith. After a long-winded answer from Dinesh, staring with "I think," Christopher makes the statement "Faith is blind." Apostle Paul disagreed and gave the definition of faith, found in Hebrews 11:1:

*"Faith is the ASSURED expectation of what is hoped for, the evident demonstration of realities that are not seen."*

**REF**

What Paul is talking about is *"convincing evidence"* not "blind faith." As an analogy, it could be likened to looking out a living room window, seeing a woman walking along holding her hat to her head with the brim folded back, papers on the street blowing past her, while leaves in the trees across the street are moving.

In your living room, looking out the window, not feeling or hearing wind, you are convinced by the demonstration of reality the wind is blowing that day. So, too, as you study your Bible, breaking free from religion and false teachings, your faith in the Bible will continue to grow.

The Bible contains letters from our creator on how best to proceed in life - very much like a manufacturer who will include a manual with his product. This manual will, when followed, gives you the best and longest use of the product. So too, the Bible, when followed, will guarantee everlasting life.

# Chapter 11

# Pray and Be Heard

Christopher asked, "Why do prayers go unanswered?"

In question 8 in the first chapter, Christopher angrily expressed how some say their prayers were answered, yet others were not. "Ridiculous" he would say. Christopher seemed to sincerely want an answer from his religious antagonists, but that answer never came.

The Bible gives sound answers as to why or why not prayers are answered. Ask yourself the following questions: Do I belong to a religious organization which tries to comply 100% with God's word and what the Bible teaches? In my religion, do I pray to a Triune God, a trinity? Do I pray to so-called saints or pray to Jesus? Am I living a life which conforms to God's will, in the Bible? Are my prayers all about me and my needs, constantly asking God only for what I want? These questions raised are just a start on answering why prayers may or may not receive an answer.

The Bible tells us God is not far off from any one of us, if we are sincere of heart, to repeat. Acts 17:27 reads,

*"...although, in fact, God is not far from each one of us."* **NIV**

Yahweh wants to have a relationship with you and encourages each one of us to come to him in prayer. Philippians 4:6 reads,

*"Don't be anxious over anything, but everything by prayer and supplication and thanksgiving, let your petitions be known to God."* **REF**

Also, Psalms 145:18:

*"LORD is near to all those calling on him, to all calling on him in truth."* **NIV**

The KJV has the name of Yahweh replaced with LORD in all capital letters. Keep in mind what Peter said at Acts 2:21, repeating the prophet Joel's words:

*"All those who call on the name of Yahweh will be saved."* **REF**

The answer to the first question you asked yourself, "Do I belong to a religious organization that is in harmony with Bible teachings?" may be a big reason why prayers go unanswered. As an example, God had a close relationship with Abraham's descendants. However, when the Israelites pulled away from God with their leaders conforming to false religion, as a group, God had nothing to do with them – and their prayers went unanswered. Isaiah 1:15 in part, says:

*"When you spread out your palms, I hide my eyes from you, although you offer many prayers, I'm not listening."* **NIV**

Very little gets through to God if you are associated with false religion. The Bible describes the type of people living today with whom God will have no part nor listen to any of their prayers, in 2 Timothy 3:1-5:

*"Know this, in the last days, people will be hard to deal with, lovers of themselves, unthankful, disloyal, lovers of money, disobedient to parents, not open to any agreement, puffed with pride, headstrong, having no natural affection, from these turn away."* **REF (Also see Galatians 5:19-21.)**

Proverbs 15:8 states:

*"The sacrifice of the wicked is detestable to God, but the prayer of the upright, is a pleasure to him."* **NIV**

For all of us to have our prayers heard by God, we must conform to his will. If we take the time to get to know the God of the Bible, he will listen to our prayers. 1 John 5:14 reads:

*"And this is the confidence we have towards him, that no matter what we ask according to his will, he will answer us."*

**NIV (Also read Mark 11:24)**

What is God's will, described in His book? It's probably not going to be your lottery ticket, or your favorite football team, or prize fighter. Those prayers may go unanswered. The Bible tells us you need no formal position to pray or speak to God. However, this does not mean being disrespectful. Remember that HE is The Sovereign Lord of the universe. You must acknowledge Jesus in every prayer ("No one comes to the father except through me,") perhaps at the beginning of your prayers, at the end, or both.

Jesus gives an illustration at Luke 11:5-8 about being *"persistent"* in our prayers. Jesus knows his father is eager to grant your request if it conforms to his will. However, you must have faith. You show your faith by being persistent in asking for what you want, by continuing to ask showing you really want what you're asking for (Luke 11:9,10).

If you have a close friend, how long would he or she remain a close friend if every time you met, you asked for something from him/her? This is the same with God! He wants to know more than just what you want; God would like to intimately know you, your feelings, the secrets in your heart, what's on your mind (good or bad), and things you love about your life. He would like to be your friend.

Christopher, in the discussions and debates, shared his disdain for praying. It was almost as if when young, he sincerely tried to reach out to God, and his prayers went unanswered. Hurt by the results, the blame in later years would fall where it should: "Man-made religion poisons everything."

# Conclusion

## What does YAHWEH want from YOU?

A question many people wonder all their lives....

*"He has told you, O man, what is good;*

*And what does Yahweh require of you. But to do justice, to*

*love kindness, and to walk humbly with your God?"*

**(Micah 6:8) NASB**

Some will consider me the mouse that roared since the lion has passed away. Right from the start, Christopher's education at the young age of eight, in the religious schools he attended, had a profound effect. Christopher wanted the truth, and had he been taught from the beginning what the Bible really teaches and not the twisted things of Christendom, we may have had the greatest advocate for faith. "Man-made religion poisons everything."

It is my hope this book has made you more familiar with your Bible and what it really teaches. Maybe this book has piqued your interest to go further in your studies? Keep in mind Jesus' words at John 17:3:

*"This means everlasting life, taking knowledge of you, the only true God and the one you sent forth, Jesus Christ."*
**NIV**

When I was a young man, I attended a baseball game with a friend. The stadium was packed with people that day, close to 50,000. Not having a father, and not really interested in sports, my mind started to wander. I started to think about police statistics and being inside the stadium with all those people. It's been said one out of a thousand is a murderer, one out of five hundred is a sex offender, one out of a hundred is a thief, and so on. I remember in conclusion thinking, "I hope we make it back to our car safely."

Why did I convey this story to you? Because all those people left the stadium that day entertained, but with no change in their lives. Just like people attending man-made false religion leave entertained, but not knowing what the Bible really teaches.

This is exactly why "Man-made religion poisons everything." The road to life, as the Bible says, is cramped and narrow and few are the ones finding it. False religion with false teachings will keep you on the broad and spacious road leading to destruction, poisoning any hope you have to get through the narrow door. 2 Corinthians 6:17 warns:

*"Therefore, get out from among them, separate yourself, says Yahweh, quit touching the unclean thing and I will take you in."* **NIV**

You have only scratched the surface of the Bible with this book. The Bible has so much more to offer you! If you have a Bible question to be answered, or would like a Bible study, please send a letter or a card to:

**"Know Your Bible" P.O. Box 12018, Newport Beach, California 92658.**

Please be sure your name and return address is included. Someone will get back to you right away.

A word of warning: as you dig deeper into the truth of what the Bible really teaches, God's adversary does not want you to know the truth and will do whatever he can to stop you.

2 Corinthians 11:4 warns God's opposer keeps turning himself into an angel of light, 1Peter 5:8:

*"Keep your senses, be watchful, your adversary, the Devil, walks about like a roaring lion, seeking to devour someone."*
**REF**

If you will, allow me to break down the following scriptures for you. (I enjoyed it when someone shared these scriptures with me.) They're found in the book of Luke 13:23-27.

*"A certain man asked, Lord are those being saved few? And Jesus tells them, to exert yourself vigorously to get through the narrow door, because many, I tell you, will seek to get in, but will not be able."*

(There are a lot of different religions out there which have not a clue about this door; Jesus is speaking to ones who know this door and call themselves Christians or Christ-like.) He goes on to say, when the householder (God) has gotten up and locked the door and you will stand outside the door, knocking saying,

*"Lord Lord open."* **REF**

But He will say to you,

*"don't know where you are from!"* **REF**

Then you will start saying,

*"We ate and drank in your presence and you taught us in the main streets,"* **REF**

(this is what Christendom is claiming) but He will say to you,

*"I don't know where you're from. Get away from me, you workers of unrighteousness."* **REF**

2 Timothy 4:3 reads: *"There will come a period of time when they will not put up with the wholesome teaching, but according to their own desire, they will surround themselves with teachers to have their ears tickled."* **REF**

If you find yourself in a religious organization that wants you to just come and have your ears tickled and give money, keep remembering the people you just read about. They didn't make it in through the narrow door for only one reason: they did not exert themselves vigorously. Keep studying your Bible. It's your life, and you will soon come in contact with those who have love for God's word. The NASB Bible at 1st John 2:17 says,

*The world is passing away, and also its lusts; but the one who does the will of God lives forever."*

Today in the United States there are over a hundred and fifty thousand laws on the books, with approximately 900 additional new laws per year being added. The first scripture quoted in this book is from Jeremiah 10: 23 and rings true,

*" it's not in man that walketh, to guide his own steps."*

Through these writings, this book has endeavored to share with you the benefits to understanding how the pieces fit.

The word of God, in fact God Himself is unchanging (Mal 3:6) If a piece of scripture doesn't 'appear' to fit, it's not because there is something wrong with His word, it's our understanding that requires adjustment, and the need for more informed study.

When Perfect man was created and placed in the garden he had one law given to him. Approximately 2200 years later the nation of Israel received 613 laws, which covered everything needed. The bible contains more answers than you can imagine in a lifetime. Continue to build your faith by knowing *WHY* you believe what you believe. YES, *WHY*?

Today there are approximately 4200 different religions around the world with many different gods. Christendom making up a large portion by numbers, perhaps the largest?

Using one book, The Bible, this religion is divided into 6 branches. Further breakdown, there are 42,000 different Christian churches using one book but teaching different man-made rules. WHY?

In John chapter 17 in prayer to Jesus Father, Jesus ask his God if He would watch over his disciples when he is gone? Jesus adds he has taught them everything he has been taught by his Father.

With this knowledge Jesus expresses, his disciples are all in agreement and speak as one, just as he and the Father are one in purpose. Jesus is speaking about the ones who would be taking part in the first Resurrection, joining him shortly in his kingdom, to rule over the Earth. However, this would also apply to all Christians to speak in unity.

If you feel you are like Christopher, not wanting to be associated with man-made false teachings, or you are one Christian trapped in one of 42,000 divisions, do as the people in our last quoted scripture found at Acts 17:11,

*"Now these were more noble-minded than those in Thessalonica, for they received the word with great*

*eagerness, examining the Scriptures daily to see whether these things were so."* **NASB**

The scripture above sets the stage, be like the Beroeans, reading the book this time looking up every scripture.

*The best to you!*

# References

- ❖ "god is Not Great: How Religion Poisons Everything," by Christopher Hitchens
- ❖ "The Faith of Christopher Hitchens," by Larry Taunton
- ❖ "War is a Racket," by Smedley Butler
- ❖ "The Truth in Translation," by Jason BeDuhn
- ❖ "The Devil's Delusion," by David Berlinski
- ❖ "Edge of Evolution," by Michael Behe
- ❖ Colliers Encyclopedia, 1986
- ❖ Vines Expository Dictionary on Old and New Testament Words, 1981 volume 2
- ❖ King James Version of the Bible, Early Edition
- ❖ Divine name King James Version of the Bible 400-year anniversary Edition
- ❖ The Reference Bible
- ❖ English Standard Version

- ❖ The American Standard Bible
- ❖ New World Translation of the Bible
- ❖ Kingdom Interlinear Greek to English
- ❖ The NIV Study Bible (New International Version)
- ❖ YouTube.com
- ❖ Smithsonian Magazine
- ❖ Time Magazine
- ❖ Catholic Bible
- ❖ United States Conference of Catholic Bishops Bible

**From Chapter 9**

***How to identify a false religion***

- ❖ Bible, a lecture entitled "Roman Pagan worship" Dr. Ryan M. Reeves, McClintock, and strong encyclopedia, eight-minute YouTube video entitled "the history of Christmas: Rome to Reformation")
- ❖ Collier's Encyclopedia
- ❖ Proverbs 14:12

# Scripture List

List of Scriptures Used, By Chapter

## Chapter One:

None

## Chapter Two:

John 17:17, 18
Luke 4:4
Matthew 23:6-12
2 Timothy 3:5, 16,17
2 Peter 1:21
Matthew 7:7
1 Thessalonians 5:21
Romans 5:12
Philippians 2:5-8
Genesis 3:19

Isaiah 44:27 - 45:3
Isaiah 13:19,20
Luke 3:15, 23-38
Daniel 9:25
Exodus 23:10,11
Nehemiah 2:1 and 5-8
Zephaniah 2:3
Revelation 7:9,13,14
1 Corinthians 10:25
Luke 23:43
1 Corinthians 11:3
Matthew 18:11
Mark 7:16
John 8:1-11
Daniel 12:4,9
John 17:3
1 Peter 2:21
John 3:17
John 14:28
Philippians 2:9
Exodus 32:
Matthew 27:52

## **Chapter Three**:

Psalms 49:7,8
Romans 5:12
Luke 1:35
Colossians 1:14
Luke 22:19,20
Ephesians 1:17
Matthew 20:28
1 Peter 1:18,19
Romans 3:23-26 and 5:6-8
1 Corinthians 1:30 and 7:23
Luke 3:23-38
2 Peter 3:8
Genesis 2:17
John 1:18
Acts 28:6
Psalms 90:2 and 90:4
Revelation 10:6
1 Timothy 1:17
Colossians 1:17
Proverbs 8:30
Psalms 36:9
Psalms 103:20
Hebrews 12:22 and 2:17
Genesis 1:1

James 1:14
Ezekiel 28:13
Revelation 12:9
1 John 5:19
Luke 4:5,6,7
Daniel 2:44
Matthew 6:9,10
Isaiah 45:18

## Chapter Four:

Genesis 3:19
Ecclesiastes 9:4
John 11:11, 14, 35
1 Corinthians 15:6
Acts 7:60
Ecclesiastes 9:5, 10
Psalms 146:4
Ecclesiastes 3:19
Ezekiel 18:4,20
Psalms 33:19 and 116:8
James 5:20
Genesis 1:3 and Genesis 4
Matthew 11:19
Luke 7:35
Romans 5:14,17, 21

Romans 6:12 and 7:8-11
1 John 5:7
1 John 4:8
Deuteronomy 32:4
Jeremiah 32:35
Genesis 2:15
Psalms 37:11,29
Hebrew 4:15 and 5:8

Galatians 5:22,23
1 Corinthians 6:9,10
Ephesians 1:5
Daniel 2:44
1 Corinthians 15:20
Matthew 11:11
John 5:28

## Chapter Five:

Hebrews 5:12
Deuteronomy 9:5
Genesis 11:6Exodus 17:8
Esther 3:1-11

## Chapter Six:

Genesis 39:9
Exodus 24:7
Matthew 5:17
Deuteronomy 9:6
Numbers 19:7-22
Leviticus 13:1-5
Deuteronomy 23:13,14
Isaiah 40:22
Job 26:7
Ecclesiastes 1:7
Matthew 7:12

## Chapter Seven:

Matthew 22 and 23
John 2:15

## Chapter Eight:

Genesis 3:15, Chapter 17 and 22:18
Hebrews 3:4
Luke 10:21
Matthew 10:34
1 Corinthians 7:19

Hebrews 12:22
Romans 2:29
Hebrews 9: 15

## Chapter Nine:

2 Corinthians 4:4
Psalms 83:18
Luke 11:1,2
Matthew 6:9
Mark 7:6-8
John 17:26
Acts 2:21 and 15:14
Acts 20:29,30
Galatians 1:8,9
1 Timothy 3:2
John 17:16

## Chapter Ten:

Hebrews 11:1

## Chapter Eleven:

Acts 17:27
Philippians 4:6

Psalms 145:18
Acts 2:21
Isaiah 1:15
2 Timothy 3:1-5
Galatians 5:19-21
1 John  5:14
Mark 11:24
Luke 11:5-8 and 11:9,10

## **Conclusion**

John 8:32 and 17:3
2 Corinthians 6:17 and 11:14
1 Peter 5:8
Luke 13:23-27
2 Timothy 4:3
Colossians 1:10
Revelation 21:3,4
Mal 3:6
Deut 4:29
1$^{st}$ Thes 5:21
Acts 17:11
Micah 6:8
Jeremiah 10:23
Malachi 3:6

Deuteronomy 4:29

Acts 17:11

# Notes

Printed in Great Britain
by Amazon